AITCH

H

John Gumbs

Published by John Gumbs
Publishing partner: Paragon Publishing, Rothersthorpe
First published 2018
© John Gumbs 2018, London

ISBN 978-1-78222-628-4

Book design, layout and production management by Into Print
www.intoprint.net
+44 (0)1604 832149

Contents

1

The Israelite Exodus

THE WEEKEND WAS drawing nigh, it was Friday and I went down to the town to do some shopping. My name is John Edonken. The time was close to 10.00 am when people started rushing hurriedly to get shelter from the pouring rain. I was close to a bookshop so I slipped in the door to avoid getting wet. As I walked passed the counter, I saw this tall blonde, blue-eyed, gorgeous, heavenly sent woman sitting behind a computer. There weren't many people in – about two or three. I felt my heart as it skipped a beat. I said to it, "Behave yourself, she could be a married woman." Straight away, I lost interest in her, the mere fact that I do not fall for women who are courting or are married or have a boyfriend. All through my life I have kept that code, and it has worked very well for me. I can sleep peacefully at nights knowing that no man is going to come and knock on my door, and to threaten me. And I can also walk safely on the streets without interference from anyone; and also too, no woman can report me to their mates because I made advances towards them. I feel so good in those areas.

I looked around in the shop and found a couple of interesting books and came to the counter to pay. She got up from behind the computer, took the books from me, checked them into the cash machine and I paid the amount with my credit card. She didn't bat an eye in a way to say that she took a fancy to me. I was just another customer. I got the strong feeling that she wasn't the type who would go round chasing men. She was there to do her job, and she did it well. I must say though, she was a friendly one. Customers would always feel pleased by the way she served them. I could have check her out some more, but as I have already said, I felt that she was another man's property. I do not mind talking to married women, or women who are courting, but to try and make them fall for me, is not at all in my books.

After paying, I took the books and left the shop. The rain had eased off and many people were again going here and there. I got to the bus stop just in time to catch my bus. Back at home, I unwrapped the books, and started browsing inside. I made myself a cuppa, nice hot chocolate, and sat down and started reading one of the two books. The author was trying to convince his readers that the Israelite Exodus actually took place. His reasoning was really first class; and he hit exactly on the subject that I was interested in. I was buried deep into the book until my belly said that it was time for food.

I went into the kitchen and knocked up something healthy. Then I continued reading the book about the Israelite Exodus.

The book said that there was one Manetho, and Egyptian priest, who wrote the history of Egypt in the Greek language. He had somewhat divided the dynasties, making the total to be around 30.

Manetho wrote that there was a king in Egypt by the name of Timaeus. At that time, men from the eastern parts came into the country with ease and took it over. They took it by force without a battle raging. Having got the people under their power, they burned down the cities, destroyed the temples of the gods. They slew many of the inhabitants, taking the children and wives, and making them slaves. The invaders made one of themselves a king.

His name was Salitis; his residence was at Memphis; he made the upper and lower regions to pay tribute. There was a place called Avaris which he made very strong, by building walls completely around it.

He placed 240,000 armed men to keep and guard it. This Salitis reigned for 13 years, then Beon took over and reigned for forty years. Then there was Apachnas who had the power for 36 years and seven months; then Apophis reigned sixty one years; and then Janius took over for 50 years and one month; after these came Assis who reigned 49 years and 2 months. These six rulers made war with the Egyptians. They were called Hyksos, Shepherd-kings. Some people say that they were Arabians. These Shepherd-kings ruled Egypt for 511 years.

The Egyptian kings who were at Thebes, decided it was time to do something; they made a long war against the Shepherds. Manetho said further that the Egyptian king Tethmosis (Ahmose), got a force of 480,000 men, and was planning to lay siege to Avaris. He gave that up, and made a treaty with the Shepherds. They were allowed to leave Egypt without anything happening to them. They can go wherever they wanted to. The Shepherds finally left with their families, about 240,000 people. They went across the desert and into Syria. They built a city in Judea, and it was called Jerusalem.

Manetho said that the slaves who worked in the quarries, after a while, approached the king that he would let them live in Avaris, the place where the Shepherds had their residence. The king Ahmose agreed to it.

When the slaves entered Avaris, they found that it was just the right place to rebel against the king. There was a man whose name was Osarsiph, a priest from Heliopolis, they took him to be their leader. The slaves swore that they will obey their leader in everything that he told them. Osarsiph had told them not to worship any of the Egyptian gods. They were told to kill the Egyptian sacred animals.

Manetho said that at this time, there were many polluted people, including some priests, who were lepers. The king of Egypt was told that he should get rid of them out of his land. It is said that the priest Osarsiph, when he became leader of the polluted slaves, his name was changed to Moses.

What I found was rather amazing. The Jewish historian Flavius Josephus wrote that the account given by Manetho of the Hyksos people, were in reality, the Jews of the Exodus.

I took hold of my bible, and went to Exodus for a read. There it said that a man from the tribe of Levi married a daughter of Levi. The woman became pregnant and brought forth a son. This son was named Moses by the Pharaoh's daughter, who found him on the bank of the river between the flags. Pharaoh, at that time, was getting rid of all the Hebrew male children by drowning them in the river. Mose's mother had hid him for three months, and then had placed him there on the river. His sister was not far away, keeping an eye on him. Then the Princess came and found him.

After reading Exodus chapter two, I let all of it sink in. According to the bible story, Moses could not be an Egyptian because he was born from parents who were both from the Levite tribe of Israel. His father was Amram, and his mother was Jochebed. He had a brother who was named Aaron, just three years older, also a sister, Miriam, who was much younger.

Weeks upon weeks, every Friday morning, I visited the bookshop. Still not one of us had really spoken in conversation to each other. The new year came, and almost at the end of that month, something rather strange took place – we actually talked to each other – and held a decent conversation. I had a couple of books in my hand and they were about Joan of Arc.

She said to me, "A very interesting woman!"

I said, "I'm doing some research on her. I want to find out how she was able to drive the English from Orleans and other places, when they were such a good disciplined and fighting army."

"Have you just started?" she asked.

"No...no, I've been doing it now for a few months."

As our conversation carried on, I learned that she wrote poems and was busy with a novel. I myself had been very busy too, jotting down poems. But I hadn't taken writing a novel seriously. I preferred to read other people's books.

"I'll let you read some of my poems when they are published. Have you been working here long?" I asked her.

"A few months ago, I started here. I do some extra work in the bib."

"Do you like this work? Or have you got your eyes on something else?"

"It's ok for the time being."

"Looking around the place I see that you have to be someone who knows what they're doing. You have to be intelligent to do this work, and behind the computer as well."

"Yes," she said, "I got the training so I'm capable of handling this sort of work."

"Does it get very busy?" I enquired.

"Some days are more busier than others. And if it gets too busy, help comes from either the boss or one of the other co-workers. And you?" she asked, checking something on the computer.

"I used to work with the students, making books for them."

"Was it hard work?"

"Very!"

"You seem to have a very good memory yourself, and very much interested in books."

"That's my area. You know, whenever I go to London, I find one of those big bookshops, and I just get lost in there. I spend hours just looking around."

"I could imagine what that's like. Staying for hours in one department!"

"They've a coffee place there so that you can relax as well. Have you ever been to London?"

"Not at all" she told me. "I heard it's a very interesting place."

"It's big. And there are so many things that you can do there. It is worth a visit."

"I suppose that I'll get the chance to see it someday."

"Have you travelled to anywhere interesting?"

"I did travel long distances, and saw some nice places ... It takes at least nine hours by plane to get to where I came from."

"Where is that?"

"Way down in the West Indies, close to USA."

"Never been down those parts!"

"The islands down there are very beautiful, and I only had the chance to see a few. On my way up, the ship docked at a place called Saint Lucia. I went into a shop to buy a postcard. I got a shock when they spoke French to me. I thought that they all spoke English. Apparently, the island belonged to France."

"That's a funny experience. What did you do when you arrived in England?"

"I was on the dole for a couple of months, until I got a job on the railways as a train cleaner, had to work three shifts then."

"Cleaning trains must have been a terrible job, all the dirt and muck!"

"Yeah! And all the grease and oil. I got home with my

coveralls reeking. But I made sure I got myself a hot soapy bath."

"Is it a nice city where you lived?"

"Yes," I answered. "It's a city in Nottinghamshire. Have you ever heard of Robin Hood?"

"I've heard the story, or I must say, the legend."

"It is a true story. He went around robbing the rich and gave it to the poor."

"He was a charitable man!"

"Oh! the Sheriff of Nottingham tried many times to catch him. The story goes back to around the 14th and 15th century where there was a yeoman living in Sherwood forest along with his men, and was always evading the Sheriff. Many people tried to find clues about this Robin Hood. Some believed that a real Robin Hood lived around the 12th century. Some say that he was a follower of King Richard."

"I have seen many films of Robin Hood, all with different actors."

"Do you know that one time I went to visit Nottingham castle, which is up on a hill, with the inn below in a grotto, someone had pinched the arrow from the Robin Hood statue that was out in front of the castle."

"Really?"

"Yes, but later, they got it back."

We talked some more about other things and then I went away to catch my bus. The next time I met her, I said to her that I would call her 'H' after she had told me what her name was. H was the first letter of her first name.

"You don't mind?" I asked her.

"Oh no, not at all. In fact I do like it, coming from you."

"One day I'll let you into the real secret why I call you 'H'."

"You are always doing that! You never tell me straight out what you actually mean. You would be telling me something, and then suddenly, you change to something else."

"I know! I realize that myself, but it's because I'm wondering if it's right at this moment to tell you straight out certain things."

"You get me interested, and then, I don't get to know anything."

"Sorry, I'll try to correct that in future."

"I know that you're a very wise man."

"Thank you," I said, "but there are billions of others wiser than myself."

"But they don't know certain things that you know. I'm amazed by some of the things you've told me."

"Have I blown your mind?"

"Just very interesting, makes me think again. By the way, there's going to be a reception next week. It's about the publication of my poems."

My face lit up, there was a smile on my face. I was absolutely thrilled to hear what she had told me.

"So you finally did it? Now you have to get your novel out; it is inside of you, you can do it."

"I'm thinking about that," she answered back. She wrote down on paper the date and the time and then gave it to me.

"I'll be very critical though when I read your poems. And if I don't like them, you know where they're going, don't you?"

She laughed and said, "In the thrash can!"

"I won't do that! Just joking. I hope that it is not too expensive to buy."

"It doesn't cost that much," she told me. "It's not a thick book or anything like that. Only 52 pages."

2

Ancient Historians

I AGREED WITH her that it was ok. I warned her that I'll be dressed in jeans, and not overdoing it. She said it was alright. We talked a lot about philosophy, religion and history. She wasn't a very strong believer and I assured her that that didn't matter.

"How's your research on Joan of Arc going?" she asked with much interest.

"Well," I said, "I'm at her birth place at the moment digging up as much information as I could find. I want my readers to know as much as they can about this girl. She is absolutely amazing!"

"You have to be careful of what you pick up on the net. Double check to see if the info is correct. There are so many sites nowadays on the net."

"You're right! I do check what I'm looking at."

"You can give me a read when you finish it." She gave a smile.

"I'll do just that."

I left the bookshop leaving H to carry on with her work. On my way home I was thinking how some of us men are really stupid. I mean we end up with a nice partner, and we don't realize it at all. H had told me that she had left her partner, and was now living by herself with her two kids – a boy and a girl. I was hoping that he doesn't come chasing after me when he finds out that I'd been talking to his wife regularly. Some men are really like that. They go absolutely beserk. I am only a customer in this bookshop, and the woman who served me turned out be one who was married. I held conversation with her which was normal in our society. If it came to the push, her husband could not point a finger to me. I was innocent, not breaking any laws. Still, I thought some more about it and was satisfied that I hadn't done anything wrong.

It was Friday evening and I went to the reception of H and her published poems. There were many people in the room, most of them teachers and writers. H's young daughter was there, I hadn't seen the young boy. She had told me that she had two children – a boy and a girl. I did see a youth in the room but I didn't connect him to H. The reception went down well, and I got a book of poems from her, along with a few words and her signature. She had to give a speech, it wasn't bad, but sometimes we had to wait for ages before she carried on with her speech, She was dressed in a red outfit, and excuse me, I'm not supposed to say this, but it is the truth, she looked gorgeous. The only time I got to talk with her was when I first came in, and when she signed the poem book. What was I expecting for God's sake? I enjoyed the reception.

Back home I started reading the poems. When I got to a certain poem, I found myself reading it over and over again. Then suddenly it came to me – the poem was about myself – visiting her every Friday, and chatting with her. I smiled and then laughed out loud. The poem was funny, the way she wrote it was very mysterious. I was the old man who came in every Friday morning. The rest of the poems went down very well, she has the knack of telling past events, setting them in verse.

When I saw H again we went into a discussion about the

Exodus, and what some of the ancient historians wrote about it. H listened attentively. She was a good listener, and she showed that she was interested to hear what I had to say.

"Stop me," I told her, "if it get too deep for you. Don't be afraid to stop me."

"I don't mind you waffling, ok! I'll stop you when I feel my mind is blowing."

"You're a brave woman," I said, "to be listening to what I'm going to say. I myself find it rather interesting, but it can blow your mind."

"I'll brace myself so that you don't blow me away."

"Okay! how funny!"

"So what did the historians write about the Jews or the Exodus?"

"I'll start with Diodorus. He was from Sicily. His full name is Diodorus Siculus. He was a Greek historian. He said that there was a plague in Egypt and they all said that it was from the gods, who were offended with them. At the time, he said, that there were many strangers and different nationalities who carried on with religious rites and ceremonies and sacrifices. The ancient manner of worshipping the gods had been abandoned and forgotten. So the Egyptians decided that the foreigners must be driven out, for they'll never be free from their miseries.

All the foreigners were put out along with some noble leaders. Some were brought to Greece and many other places. The most famous of their leaders were Danaus and Cadmus. The great majority of the foreigners went into a country not far from Egypt, which is called Judea, it had no inhabitants at that time. The leader of these people was one Moses, a very wise and valiant man."

H broke in,

"So the bible was right when it talked about Moses?"

"Yes," I said. "Diodorus has the name of Moses in his history."

"Go on," H said, "let's hear some more."

"Diodorus said that Moses took possession of the country, amongst other cities, built that most famous city Jerusalem, and the temple there."

"Wasn't it Solomon who build the temple?" H asked.

"That's what the bible said, but you know those ancient historians, they get their stories all mixed up. At least he mentioned that there was a 'Moses.'"

"From what I've read," H stated quite clearly, "it was Solomon, the son of David who built the temple, and not Moses. Moses did get instructions from God to build the 'Tabernacle' in the wilderness."

"You're right, H," I told her, "Diodorus is only relating what he picked up from other writers."

"What else did he write?"

"He said that Moses instituted the holy rites and ceremonies with which they worshipped God; and made laws for the the government of the state. He also divided the people into twelve tribes."

"It was Moses who gave the Israelites their laws," H told me as she walked over to the coffee machine and got herself a cup of hot coffee. "It was God who gave the Ten Words along with other laws."

"And here I am thinking that you no nothing about the bible."

"I've a bible that I read now and then."

"Well, you know what you're saying."

"What more did Diodorus say?"

"He said that Moses said that the number 12 was a perfect number; and also because it corresponds to the 12 months of the year."

H looked a bit uneasy as she said, "Surely it was from Jacob that the 12 tribes came from. Joshua carried out the distribution of the land according to what God and Moses had said."

"We shall carry on with this discussion at another time. I have to get these tax papers to the tax office."

I said so long to H and left the bookshop.

H is a very interesting woman. She listens to everything I have to say, even if she doesn't know anything about it. You do not find that with many people. I got to the tax office and waited around for about half an hour, then I went and sat at the desk of a man who would examine my papers. After that, I left, took a bus and went home.

At home I was thinking of a few detective books that I had read; and in each one, they made the blonde woman to be dumb. H was blonde, but she wasn't dumb. She was clever, she was an intelligent woman. I remembered that she told me she was teaching young children in a part time job. She doesn't appear dumb to me, and working in that big bookshop, shows that she wasn't dumb at all. She knew quite a lot as well. But I, being one who likes to tease, jokingly, I could have talked to her as if she was a dumb blonde, but I knew before hand that it would not go down well.

I could remember too that I had a discussion with H and we were talking about blondes, and we came on the subject of 'dumb blondes'. H had said, "I'm no dumb blonde"; we both laughed.

While at home, I read some more on Flavius Josephus, the Jewish historian. Nero, the emperor, had sent Flavius Vespasian to Judea to stop the rebellion. The Jews were rampaging against Roman rule. Vespasian had a son whose name was Titus, and was also a good commander. Vespasian was to take charge of the 5th and 10th legions in Syria, while his son would get together the 15th legion in Egypt and march it to meet up with him.

Josephus was in charge of the forces in Galilee. He was captured at Jotapata. When he was brought before Vespasian and Vespasian son, he predicted that Vespasian would become Emperor. Strangely enough, after four emperors died quickly one after the other, Vespasian became Emperor, he released Josephus and had him adopted into the Vespasian family, and Josephus became Flavius Josephus.

Just before capture, Josephus was involved with his own soldiers who made a suicidal pact. The 41 soldiers decided that they would form a circle. Then the first man chosen, would then have to kill the man on his left, this carried on until there was only one man left. That last man would then have to kill himself. It is stated that Josephus didn't want to lose face and surrender to the Romans. He placed himself in a position in the circle of his comrades, where he knew he would be the last one remaining.

Joseph ben Mattathias was his Jewish name. He was a priest, scholar and historian, and was born in AD 37.

When he was young, around the age of 14, according to his own account, the Jewish priests came to him in concern with Jewish law When he was 16, he went and stayed in the wilderness with a hermit whose name was Bannus. Josephus became a Pharisee. In AD 64 he took a trip to Rome trying to release some jewish priests who were prisoners. Nero's second wife, Poppaea Sabina helped him in his mission and everything went well. He liked what he saw there in Rome, their culture and the way they organize themselves.

In AD 66 the Jews revolted against Roman rule encouraged by the Zealots. Josephus was made military commander of Galilee. Josephus had held the fortress of Jotapata for 47 days,

40,000 inhabitants were slaughtered when the city fell. He had taken refuge in a deep cave with another 40 soldiers where they had made the suicidal pact instead of giving themselves up to the Romans.

H was away for four weeks on her holidays. I would be a liar if I said that I didn't miss her. Of course, I did miss her, and our weekly chat.

She saw me when I walked through the door; her eyes lit up; she was pleased to see me again; and so was I, to see her again too. Now if we were close, and she wasn't married, I would have grabbed her, and given her a big hug. Instead, I just held her hand and welcomed her back.

She started stacking books in the book rack when she said, "How was your time?"

"You know me, I watched a few films, did some work on the computer, went out for walks, and that was it."

"I went for walks with my dogs," she told me, "and relaxed quite a lot."

"Dogs?"

"Oh! I have another one. Now I have two." She took her mobile and started showing me pictures.

"Lovely," I said. "I love dogs very much, lucky you!"

"How's your writing coming on? Have you written any poems?" She was interested to know.

"Many plots keep coming to me, and all I can do is grab my pen, and do some writing. The poems are strange and unusual. I just write them down as they come into my head."

"You have a way with your poems, they tell a historical story, of events, you know what I mean?"

"And you? How's your writing coming on? Last time we talked, you were thinking about a novel."

"I started it but I had to put it aside for the moment. I just couldn't think at the time."

"Some writers do get that, but it will all come to you again."

"I have to make sure that I finish it in time for the publishers."

"Don't worry," I said, "you can do it. It's all there inside of you."

"I'll just wait for the time when it all starts to flow again."

"Is it going to be an interesting novel?"

"You'll have to wait until it's finish and published before you can have a read."

"Then I'll just have to wait."

"Have you found anything more about the Exodus? H wanted to know. Any more writers besides Diodorus?"

I looked at her, still stacking books, and said,

"There's this Lysimachus. He was one of those who didn't like the Jews and tried to slander them. Josephus, who read Lysimachus' history about the Jews in Egypt wasn't at all very pleased. He wrote that Lysimachus told many lies."

"This history business is interesting but you have to be good when trying to unravel what is true and what isn't."

I said to H, "I don't mind digging in, I have to wade through quite a lot. Do you know I almost broke down and cried when I read what the Romans did to the Alexandrian Library. About 700,000 volumes of books got burned. Even now, it still hurts."

"That's a lot of books," H said. "God knows what was written therein."

"They weren't thinking of us future ones. They would torch anything that was in sight belonging to the enemy."

H said, "I read somewhere that it was accidentally destroyed by Julius Caesar around 48 BC."

"H," I said, "you're right. It started with the enemy. Reports said that the enemy tried to destroy the fleet of Julius Caesar but he retaliated by using fire. This got out of hand and spread to the library."

H finished stacking the books in the racks and went and had herself a cup of coffee. She knew that I didn't drink tea or coffee, and there was no point in offering me a cup. She asked if I wanted some water. I said, no thanks. She was now seated behind the computer. She looked up at me, where I was standing by the counter, where the cash machine was.

She said, "So Josephus found what Lysimachus wrote damaging to the Jews? Did he make it clear who the Jews really were?"

I said to her, "Here is what Josephus said:"

I shall now add to these accounts about Manetho and Cheremon somewhat about Lysimachus, who has taken the same topic of falsehood with those afore mentioned, but has gone far beyond them in the incredible nature of his forgeries; which plainly demonstrates that he contrived them out of his virulent hatred of our nation. His words are these:

'The Jewish people being leprous and scabby, and subject to certain other kinds of diseases, in the days of Bocchoris, king of Egypt, they fled to the temples, and got their food there by begging: and as the numbers were very great that were fallen under these diseases, there arose a famine in Egypt. Whereupon Bocchoris, the king of Egypt, sent some to consult the oracle of Ammon about this famine. The god's answer was this, that he must purge his temples of impure and impious men, by expelling them out of those temples into desert places; but as to the scabby and leprous people, he must drown them, and purge his temples, the sun having an indignation at these men being suffered to

live; and by this means the land will bring forth its fruits. Upon Bocchoris having received these oracles, he called for their priests, and the attendants upon their altars, and ordered them to make a collection of the impure people, and to deliver them to the soldiers, to carry them away into the desert; but to take the leprous people and wrap them in sheets of lead, and let them down into the sea.

Whereupon the scabby and leprous people were drowned, and the rest were gotten together, and took counsel what they should do, and determined that, as the night was coming on, they should kindle fire and lamps, and keep watch; that they also should fast the next night, and propitiate the gods, in order to obtain deliverance from them.

That on the next day there was one Moses, who advised them that they should come to places fit for habitation: that he charged them to have no kind regards for any man, nor give good counsel to any, but always to advise them for the worst; and to overturn all those temples and altars of the gods they should meet with: that the rest commended what he had said with one consent, and did what they had resolved on, and so travelled over the desert.

But that the difficulties of the journey being over, they came to a country inhabited and that there they abused the men, and plundered and burned their temples; and then came into that land which is called Judea, and there they built a city, and dwelt therein, and that there city was named Hierosyla, from this their robbing of the temples; but that still, upon the success they had afterwards, they

in time changed to its denomination that it might not be
a reproach to them, and called the city Hierosolyma, and
themselves Hierosolymites.

"That piece of history sounds a bit confusing," H said. "The king Bocchoris was in power around 722 BC. His Egyptian name is Bakenranef, known to the Greeks as Bocchoris."

"Again, H, you've hit the nail on the head," I said to her. "It's like a history war going on between the Greeks and the Jews. Each trying to prove that their nation came to be from a long time ago. Josephus wrote that the Greeks are recent, and that the Jews are ancient."

"But what have Bocchoris to do with Moses?" H asked, looking confused. "He was a king of the 24th dynasty, and known as a law giver."

"There were a few law givers who gave written codes for govenmental constitution. Moses is also one of them – for the Jewish nation."

I had a quick look around to see if any new books came in, I found none. I said so long to H, left the bookshop and went to the baker's.

On the way there, I began to think about some of those ancient historians who got their stories in the wrong era. They were reporting what they had found in the history of their nation, but sometimes added a bit more. And I was thinking too, why didn't the bible mention the name of the Pharaoh who took Abram's wife Sarai, into his harem. Things would have worked out much easier, and one would have had a good timeline to work with. It could have even mention the Pharaoh by name of the Exodus. All we read is: *"The King of Egypt, the Pharaoh."* The bible gave the names of two cities or store houses – Pithom and Ramesses. One interesting point was: *"There was a new king who did not know about Joseph."* I was thinking very hard about that. I was trying to fit Joseph in the Amarna period, then up to Horemheb, the general who became Pharaoh. He got rid of all the writings he could find about the Amarna kings, so that the next king after him, Ramesses I, would not know anything about Joseph. But there was one problem – there was no famine in the Amarna period.

It is reported that there was a famine in the time of Amenemhet III. Moses was supposed to be Amenemhet IV, and had served along with his step-father for 9 years, then he disappeared. He was about 30 when he started reigning with his step-father. Then when his step-father died, there was no one to take the throne but his daughter Sobekneferu. After her reign, the 12th dynasty came to an end.

There are so many reports about Moses, and I do take time to go through them to see what I could find. Then we have the report of Artapanus setting Moses in a time when there were many kings ruling. I had the strong feeling that Moses fitted in around the Ramesses family. I do not think that Ramesses II was the Pharaoh of the Exodus. He was too powerful to be overthrown by Moses. But the bible said that it was God who overthrew the Pharaoh and his army through Moses and Aaron. I was thinking of Merneptah as the Pharaoh of the Exodus. I read that a stele had been found with the name of Israel on it dated around 1200 BC.

3

The Artapanus history of Moses

THE NEXT WEEK I saw H again. She said to me that she had something that she knew I would like.

I asked her, "What is it?"

She showed me a new book about Joan of Arc. I was delighted.

"You really know what I like. Can't wait to get stuck in."

"Any new discovery on the Exodus?" H asked me. "Have you got the name of the Pharaoh?"

"That's a very hard thing, H. I'm working on it. Writers have given who they think was the Pharaoh, but I place them aside for the moment."

"It's getting really difficult. I think you need to stay with the bible story. There is some truth therein. For why should it say that Joseph was sold into Egypt if it wasn't so. Why would it say that Abram went down to Egypt if it wasn't so. Or Jacob entering with his family. The story has to be true. It is just the time period."

"You know, I'm working on that as well. But God! there are so many dates. I even found some dates from Nostradamus. I'm looking at them very carefully. I'm also working on dates to do with Seti I. Some Jewish writings give the name of Bithia, the princess who saved Moses. Seti I had a sister who was named Tia. There's a problem here though."

"What is that?" H asked.

"Seti had a son, and the Pharaoh we're looking for, only had a daughter."

"I see," H remarked. "So you have to dig through the Pharaohs to see who had what? What a task you have taken on. I wish you all the best there."

"Tell me something," I said to her, "about your novel. How's it coming on?"

"I'm nearing the end. I started writing and I just couldn't stop. Really amazing!"

"I told you it would come flowing back again."

"I hope the publishers would be pleased with it and not throw it in the thrash can."

"They won't do that. Not a novel from H. They have to publish it. What do you think yourself? Were you pleased with the way you wrote it?"

"Yes, I felt that it was written ok."

"How's everything else? I do hope fine."

She looked up at me, and was probably surprised that I asked her that.

"Not bad at all, could be better. Thanks for asking!"

"That's normal. Just want things to go well for you."

"Thanks again!"

"Have you been working hard here, many customers?"

"Now and then I get quite a few, and at other times, it's as if the shop doesn't exist."

"You know when I was young, I did work in shops, and I told myself that I will never go into business that has to do with a shop or restaurant. It is hard work to start with, and working all hours of the day."

"That's true! it's hard work and sometimes not much profit."

"Lucky are the ones who make it work without losing," I said. "They can show a big smile."

"Your book on Joan of Arc," H said, "is it difficult? And how far are you with it?"

"I'm nearly finished, just a couple chapters to go. It is much easier than the Exodus. Quite a lot has been written about her with many eye witnesses."

"That was quick. I wish I were that quick in writing a novel, I would have had quite a few out by now."

"The Exodus is going to take a long time to write. I think that Josephus has quite a lot to say in his histories. It is Artapanus, he gives the name of the Pharaoh of Moses as Khaneferre (Sobekhotep IV). He was a king of the 13th dynasty. This dynasty had a number of kings who only reigned for a short time."

"What if Artapanus is wrong? He gives the name of the daughter of the Pharaoh who saved Moses as 'Merris.'"

"Yes, that's what he wrote. Josephus said it was 'Thurmutis.'"

"Sounds like Tuthmosis."

"Or Artapanus could have meant Joseph, being Governor around the 12 or13 dynasties. These writers are always getting their names mixed up."

H wanted to know what else did Artapanus write about Khaneferre.

"You sure you want to hear all this?"

"Go on," H said, "I might be able to pick something out of it."

"Artapanus did give the name of the king of Egypt as Pharethothes whom Abram met. He said that Abram taught him astrology, and that Abram stayed in Egypt for 20 years. Artapanus calls the son of Abram Mempsasthenoth, and the son of the king of Egypt, he called Palmanothes."

"Why didn't he give the Hebrew names?" H wanted to know.

"He was writing the history for the Greeks, that's why the Greek names."

"Is there more?" H asked.

"Yes, lots more. Artapanus wrote that Palmanothes took over when his father died, and that he treated the Jews in a bad way. He got a daughter Merris, and gave her as wife to Chenephres (Khaneferre) who was king of the regions above Memphis. Merris was barren and adopted a Hebrew child, and called his name Mouses (Moses): the Greeks called him Musaeus when he was grown up. They said that this Moses was the teacher of Orpheus."

"I've heard the story of Orpheus," H told me. "He had a way of moving stones and trees by his songs. He went down to the underworld to get his dead wife back from Pluto."

"Did he manage to get her back?" I asked.

"If I remembered rightly, Eurydice was his wife. One day she was going through some tall grass when she was bitten by a snake and died. Orpheus mourned for her then decided to fetch her from Hades. He descended singing his songs. It is said that the spirits wept. He persuaded Persephone to help him bring back to life his dead wife. Pluto had no choice but to let her go. Orpheus promised Pluto that he would not look back, on his way up, until he came to his house. Orpheus, as he neared the entrance, looked back to see if his wife was there, but she fell back into Hades, and so he came back without her. There are many different versions to the story."

"Nice sad story. These mythological stories has secrets in them. You need to find what the secret is."

"When we compare what Artapanus wrote and what Josephus wrote, and what is stated in the bible, they all differ from each other. Sometimes Artapanus is correct with what the bible says, and sometimes he's way on his own describing events which are not in the bible or Josephus. He states that when the Israelites were crossing the Red sea, that it was a stream, and that Moses knew about the ebb and tide. He also said that when the Egyptians went in after the Israelites that a fire was seen in the path along with a flood."

"Interesting, that part," I told H. "Moses talked a lot about the fire of God, and how the Israelites don't have to do anything, God would fight for them and destroy their enemies."

"You know," H said, "Josephus said that Moses smote the sea with his rod, which parted asunder at the stroke, leaving a dry path for the Hebrews. He said that when the Egyptian army went into the sea, it flowed back to its own place, and there was a torrent raised by storms of wind and surrounded the Egyptians. Showers of rain came down from the sky, and there was dreadful thunders and lightning, with flashes of fire. Thunderbolts also came upon them. The night was dark and dismal. He said that they all perish, and that there was not one man left to be a messenger of the calamity to the rest of the Egyptians."

"But surely," I said, "the rest of the Egyptians would have been eager to know what happened. They must have known that the army went out against the Israelites. When no one came back, they would have sent people out looking. The bible said that the dead bodies of the Egyptians had come ashore, and the Israelites had armed themselves."

"Strangely enough," H told me, "Artapanus wrote that there was a flash of fire in the path behind the Israelites. I think that we have to take some things he wrote very seriously, others, we just put aside for later."

"I don't know what to really say or think about this Artapanus. His story about Moses is strange. This is what he wrote:"

He said that Moses divided the state into 36 nomes, and appointed a god to be worshipped by each nome. Moses did quite a lot of things to keep Knaneferre safely in power. He said that the people loved Moses, and that the priests honored him as a god, and was named 'Hermes', because of his interpretation of the hieroglyphics. Khaneferre became jealous of Moses and tried to kill him. Then later, the Ethiopians invaded Egypt. Khaneferre sent Moses in command of an army against the Ethiopians. The troops of Moses were mainly farmers, most weak and unable to fight. But Moses with 100,000 men came to Hermopolis. Artapanus wrote that the people of Heliopolis stated that the war lasted for 10 years. So Moses built a city for his army – he called it "Hermes City." He, Artapanus said that the Ethiopians became so fond of Moses, that they even learned circumcision from him. When the war was ended, Khaneferre pretended to welcome Moses, still secretly plotting against him.

Artapanus wrote too, that Khaneferre hired Chanethothes to get rid of Moses. Moses was informed before hand. Around this time Merris died and was buried by Moses. Moses called the city and the river by the name of "Meroe." Merris, Artapanus wrote, was highly honored by the people. Now he says that Aaron, the brother of Moses knew about the plot, and told Moses to go away to Arabia. Chanethothes found out about Moses' departure and laid an ambush for him. He failed to kill Moses, and Moses killed him, and made his escape to Arabia and stayed with Raguel, the ruler of the district. Moses later married his daughter. This Raguel wanted to make an attack on the Egyptians, but Moses forbade him. Artapanus has

*fire suddenly coming from the earth when there was no
wood or fuel around, Moses took flight when he saw it but
a divine voice spoke to him, that he must march against
Egypt, and bring the Jews out back to their old country.*

"Shall I carry on," I asked H.

"I don't mind," she answered. "But he's far out, compared to
what is written in the bible."

"That's quite true. Artapanus goes on to say that Moses
took a force against the Egyptians:"

*He first met his brother Aaron. The King of Egypt called
Moses before him, wanting to know what he came back
for. Moses said the Lord of the World commanded him
to deliver the Jews. When the king heard this, he shut
Moses up in prison. But when it was night, all the doors
of the prison-house opened of their own self, some of the
guards died, and others were fast asleep with their weapons
broken in pieces. Moses went out and entered the palace,
finding the doors open.*

*The guards were all in deep sleep. Moses woke up the king,
and he, the king being amazed, asked Moses to tell him
the name of the God who sent him. Moses whispered in
the king's ear. When he heard what Moses said, he became
speechless. Moses held him fast and he came to life again.
Moses wrote the name in a tablet and sealed it up; and
one of the priests who made light of what was written in
the tablet was seized with a convulsion and died. The king
asked Moses to work some sign for him, and Moses threw
down the rod which was in his hand, and it turned into a
serpent. And when they were all frightened, Moses seized it*

by its tail, and it became a rod again. Then he went forth and smote the Nile with his rod, and the river became flooded and deluged the whole of Egypt. The water was stagnant and stank and killed all living things in the river, and the people were perishing of thirst.

The king said that after a month he would let the people go, if Moses would restore the river to its proper state. Moses smote the river again with his rod, and checked the stream. The king summoned the priests from above Memphis, and said that he would kill them all, and demolish the temples, unless they also would do some wonder. And they by some witchcraft and incantations. made a serpent, and changed the color of the river.

Now the king started showing his power by maltreating the Jews with every kind of vengeance and punishment. Then Moses did other signs. Striking the earth and bringing forth a kind of winged animal to harass the Egyptians, and all their bodies broke out in boils. The Egyptian physicians could not heal the people. Moses, with his rod brought up frogs, locusts and lice. And for this reason, the Egyptians dedicated the rod in every temple, and to Isis likewise, because the earth is Isis, and sent up wonders when smitten by the rod. The king still persisted in his folly.

Moses cause hails and earthquakes by night at that time, most of the houses fell in, and most of the temples. The king at last let the Jews go; and they after borrowing from the Egyptians many drinking-vessels, and raiment, and very much other treasure, crossed the rivers on the Arabian side, and after a long journey, came on the third day to the Red sea. The people of Memphis say that Moses been acquainted with the country, waited for the ebb, and took the people across the sea when dry. But the people of Heliopolis say that the king hastened after them with a great force.

A divine voice came to Moses telling him to strike the sea with the rod, and so the stream divided, and they passed over by a dry path. When the Egyptians went in with them, a fire, it is said. shone out upon them from the front, and the sea overflowed the dry path, and the Egyptians were all destroyed by the fire and the flood: but the Jews, having escaped this danger spent forty years in the wilderness. God rained down food for them. Moses, they say was tall and ruddy, with long white hair, and dignified. And he perfomed these deeds when he was 89 years old.

"Now after listening to that," H told me, "I feel that he left out quite a lot. He didn't mention that Moses had two sons, but he did mention that he got married. It seems also that he deliberately bypass many things of what Josephus said. If he read Josephus, why didn't he report that Moses married a Cushite wife. In the bible, we read of Miriam and Aaron confronting Moses because of this."

"I've read that too. Why didn't he report that Moses came upon a burning bush, and that the bush wasn't burning even though it was on fire? He just mentioned that there was a fire that came out of the ground. I wonder if he had a copy of the bible?"

H said, "Ptolemy II had the Hebrew scriptures set over into Greek by 70 scribes. Artapanus, being an Alexandrian of Jewish Egyptian descent, must have had access to the Hebrew scriptures."

"I think so too," I replied. "You have to take it all with a pinch of salt. Manetho did say that the Hebrews were the Hyksos who were in Egypt for a long time."

"Tell me more about the Hyksos," H said. "Were they Syrians, Arabs or Phoenicians?"

"The Hyksos were Asian people who invaded Egypt and made their capital at Avaris. They were actually known as 'Rulers of foreign countries.'"

"And their gods?"

"They had their own gods, they honored some of the Egyptian gods, like Seth. They took power from the 13th dynasty kings bringing the 15 dynasty into being. It was they who brought the chariot and the war-horse. They didn't rule Egypt completely."

"Were there really many kings ruling in the 13th dynasty. And is it possible to fit Joseph in that dynasty?" H asked.

"Manetho, though he made some mistakes gave a history of about 60 kings ruling the 13th dynasty."

"Wow! So many?"

I said, "Yes, there are quite a few of them listed; and Amenemhet 6th could be the Pharaoh of Joseph. You have done well by asking me certain questions. I am glad I have you around. You're not just a pretty face you know. You're a great help to me, and what I'm researching is not your subject."

H answered, "I like looking up bits and pieces on the net and if I find anything interesting, I note it down and ask you questions on it."

"That's clever, but don't ignore your own notes for your future novels."

"I won't! I'm just waiting to see what the publishers will do with that first novel. Sometimes I'm worried."

"Take it easy," I said. "It will be ok!"

"I hope so!"

"Another time," I said, "we'll talk about some more ancient writers."

"That's fine," H agreed, and I left her busying herself sticking prices on books she had just taken out of a cardboard box. A few customers came in just as I was leaving.

4

Joseph, Joking with H, Astrology

OUTSIDE IT WAS a bit wet, it had been raining for about an hour, and the sun was now trying to peek through the grey dark -clouds. I went around and did some shopping. I had a quick look at the computer shop to see what was new there. A lot of second hand computers, and going cheap. Well, to me, it was cheap, but I was forgetting that not so long ago, the currency had changed from Guilders to Euros. I asked a few questions about why the computer behaved in a certain way, and was satisfied with the answers I got. I spent a few minutes looking around quickly in a jeans shop, then I strolled down to the bus stop.

Safely home, I dug into something tasty, switched the computer on and started browsing. I was interested in finding something more about Moses and the Exodus. I skipped over a few sites, and came to one that was very good. I read through a bit and was glad that I did so. It talked about Artapanus and how he related his story about Moses, it was other writers who wrote about what Artapanus said. His original work wasn't around any more – only fragments remained. I started making notes and found some dates very interesting. After that, I quickly looked at the story of Joseph and Asenath. I have read a lot of apocryphal works hoping to find some clues within them.

This one about Joseph and Asenath relate how Joseph called the Pharaoh, at that time, his father. When he was offered Asenath as his wife by her father Petephres, Joseph said that his father, the Pharaoh, will give her to him. The Pharaoh had a son who also wanted Asenath as his wife. This Asenath was very beautiful, she was an Egyptian according to the story, and she worshipped Egyptian gods. Joseph was a man of the God of Israel, he did not worship idols, but I found this part strange for him to be marrying an Egyptian. Another part of the story says that the Pharaoh's son tried to get Joseph's brothers to join him in order to kill Joseph, so that he could marry Asenath.

The story said that when the Pharaoh died that the crown went to Joseph, and that he was king over Egypt for 48 years, after which Joseph grandson took over. Does that sound strange to you? The king of Egypt would just hand his crown over to an Israelite? The Egyptians were very protective about the crown and who gets it. They rarely let an outsider get the crown. Sometimes they would marry their own sisters or brothers to keep the power within the family.

There's something really interesting written in the bible. At the age of 30, Joseph stood before the King, some think that it could have been Amenemhat 6th, others say it was Amenhotep I, and that Amenhotep III was the Pharaoh who knew not Joseph. In the bible, we are told that the Pharaoh made Joseph Master of Egypt, he was the next highest apart from the king. The Pharaoh gave Joseph his signet ring, and a gold chain was placed around his neck. Joseph rode in a second chariot next to Pharaoh. This is taking me back to when Horemheb was in power with Tutankhamen as king. But how could Joseph's grandson take the crown of Egypt? There's only one way where that was possible. Joseph must have had a daughter who married the Pharaoh, and a son must have been born. We are told that Joesph had two sons – Manasseh and Ephraim. That's enough for now, I said to myself. So I switched on the TV and relaxed myself.

I met H again and she was in a happy mood. I walked over to the counter and said, "Hello, H, you look as if you have won the lottery."

"I wish I had," she said, "it would have come in pretty handy."

"Lucky are those whose laps it falls in," I told her. "In this life you have to take the chance when it comes round."

"Is there another life then?"

"It's just something I read. I can't say really what it's all about."

"How's everything going for you?" H asked.

"I'm still breathing strong. I can't complain."

Suddenly the phone rang. H picked it up and began talking, when she was finished, she didn't look at all pleased.

"Is there something wrong?" I asked her.

She said, "It's the school. It's my son. He's not attending to his lessons."

"Sometimes that happens, and they get over it. Don't worry much about it, things will come good again."

"I hope so," she said, "because he's a nice boy, he never gives any trouble."

"So you have to go to school and be told off by his teacher?"

H smiled, found what I said funny. "Have you done any writing on Joan of Arc?"

"It is finished," I told her. "I just need to go through it and see if it makes any sense."

"Good for you," she told me. "Now you have to find yourself a publisher."

"I will do that. I will get in contact with one. But you know it's not going to be easy for a first time unknown writer. I once read a book which was first class, and it was turned down in the beginning by many publishers."

"You still have to send yours away," H urged me, "they might like it straight away."

"I don't think that I'm that lucky. I prefer reading other people's books than to be writing one. It has to be written well for the publishers to take it."

"Last time I saw you," H said, "you mentioned that you were also studying astrology."

"I've been looking at it now for the last 40 years."

"What do you see? Or I must ask, what's it all about?"

"It's just an ancient science," I told her. "It's a chart showing the positions of the heavenly bodies at the time of one's birth."

"Heavenly bodies?" H wanted me to tell her more.

"Planets," I told her.

"Ok! if I give you my birth data, what can you tell me?"

"I'm not a real astrologer. I'm only a researcher, but I can tell you what the planets are doing to each other at a certain time. They're sometimes positive and negative to each other, and that does affect the individual."

H gave me her birth data, and also of her son and daughter.

"I will draw up a chart for each one of you and try to explain simply how it works."

H said, "I'm intrigued by it all. Can't wait!"

"What I'm going to show you is not all there is to it. It is very deep and complex."

"It's new to me. I'm nosy. I want to see if it makes any sense."

"In time you'll see what makes sense and what doesn't."

It was time again to leave H, and to let her get on with her work. H was a very interesting woman. She wants to know how things work, and it must be explained to her very clearly, or else she gets completely upset. I told her that I will try my very best to explain to her about this astrology business. I knew before hand that it was not going to be an easy matter.

Explaining astrology to some one who doesn't know anything at all about it, is a tough job. I have to prepare myself for that. I went to the shop and bought myself a few postcards; it was the month for many birthdays in my family. It was past midday when I arrived back home.

While I had been doing research on Joan of Arc and writing the book, an idea popped in to my head. The knights code had to do with bravery, courtesy, honor and gallantry toward women. I picked out two of them: to speak the truth at all times, and to respect the honor of women. All the codes I like, but these two, I knew that H saw them very deeply wrapped up inside of me.

Now I decided to get myself a charger and dressed myself up as a knight. H wouldn't be able to recognize me with the face piece on.

It was easy to hire a horse for the day, and the armour, I got from a carnival dress shop. When the day came to present myself in armour to H, I got a few people to help me with putting the armour on, and getting on the horse. It was really strange and daunting. In the town, people rarely ever see horses, except the ones the police control the crowds with, and the two big horses that now and then pulled the beer wagon through the town. People were staring when they saw me. At this time I was heading up the street where the old Post Office building was situated. At times I felt a bit uncomfortable, and I was thinking of Joan of Arc and those other knights, riding for hours on end without complaining. Well they were accustomed to it, and I was only doing it for a laugh. I wonder what H would think when she saw the horse, and me coming through the door dressed to the toes in armour. Would she burst out laughing or would she be curious to know what the heck was at hand?

As I walked through the door, she saw me because she was behind the computer and had a good view of both entrances to the shop.

She said as she got up from her seat, "What have we got here now? You've really gone and done it. You're indeed mad! Only you would do such a thing as this!"

I lifted my visor up, then said, "Madam, you're welcome! I'm pleased to be of service to you, and for your safety."

"For safety, you'll need to have more than one knight."

"I'm many in one," I said to her. "I'm the knight you've always dreamt of."

"I've never dreamt of a knight in my life. But you're funny! going through all that just for me. I knew it was you. I knew it!"

"I had to do it because the idea had been haunting me for a long while. I thought,can it actually be done? And sure enough, here I am."

"You're brave as well. Not many men these days would have done that. Kneel down and let me make you a real knight."

"I should have been back in the Middle Ages, it would have gone down well. And if I was in Joan of Arc's group, my, that would have been great."

"This is the 21st century and you have to accept it."

"Before I go," I said to H, "I have to do one last thing."

"What is it? I hope that it's nothing foolish."

"Oh no," I took her hand, and knelt on one knee. "It's just an honourable act." Then I kissed her hand.

"It's a nice gesture, but it is still mad, coming here on a horse in armour."

"I'm the knight of the 21st century!"

Mad or not, I was pleased that I had pulled it off. If the knights in the medieval ages could do it, why couldn't I? I felt much better now that it was all behind me. To tell you the truth, I have another idea, but that is for later. When the armour and horse were returned, and I was home, a smile came on my face.

"How dare you?" I said to myself. "How dare you?"

The next week I entered the bookshop and H was in a happy mood. Her novel had been taken to the publishers. She now had to wait and see what the result would be. We talked about what I had done; the knight business.

I said to her, "I want to be reading your novel. I hope it won't take too long before it's out."

"I hope so too," she said. "But I have to wait and see what they're going to do with it."

"Maybe..."

"No, no. You're thinking that they might turn it down."

"I was just going to say, maybe they forgot about it."

"Publishers don't forget about a manuscript, unless it's that bad. And anyway, they would have sent it back to you. Just relax and wait."

"Ok!"

"Take good care, see you later."

"Bye for now!"

When I left H, I was already planning another adventure. I really wanted to see how she'd take this second one. I got myself a golden retriever and started training it. I would talk to it daily as if it was a human being. The training was coming on ok. H had it in her mind that I didn't like dogs. This came about from chats we had before. I had asked her what breed were her dogs. She would smile and say to me that she had rescued them. Little did she know that I was a great lover of dogs.

There was one time when I was living in Germany. I had a black labrador that had been given to me by a family who was leaving to go back to England. I started training the dog to play football, and it was so good that the children in the area used to come and ask if they could play with my dog.

This golden labrador was a treat, its behaviour was fantastic. When I was ready for this adventure, I took the dog to the town. I showed it the bookshop where H was working – book stands outside – and lining the entrance. As I have already said, the bookshop had two entrances. After the dog had seen the first entrance, I took it to the second one.

I said to it, "You'll go to the first entrance, with this note that I shall put around your neck. You shall open the doors because they're are easy to open, with just a slight push, and then, she would see you, and then come to you, and see the note."

The dog barked a few times, and I knew it understood what I said. I patted it a few times, then I continued, "Now I will go through the second door. Now this is important," I said to the dog, as I stooped down next to it, "you have to pretend that you don't know me when I walk in. Don't let her know that you're my dog."

The second door was a heavy door and it was impossible for the dog to open it. The first door which is facing the Old post office was much easier. It had a sort of sliding door which stayed open during working hours. Then there was another door that was like saloon doors, only taller. The dog could easily make its way through these.

On the day when H was on duty, she brought out some low tables, with books on them at the first entrance. She started hoovering a bit around. She then set the computer on and checked the e-mails. There were a couple of sealed boxes with new books. She opened the first one, and took some books out, checking them. She placed price stickers on them. She was on the left of the cash machine when she heard the noise of the swing doors opening. She was surprised when she saw the golden retriever come into the shop.

She saw immediately the note that was attached to its collar. She moved from behind the counter and walked to meet the dog. It was wagging its tail furiously, and she saw how friendly the dog was. She took the note from the collar and started to read:

My master has great respect for you. He thinks that you are an angel.

Her face lit up, then she said to the dog,

"Who is your master?"

I waited another ten minutes, then I came through the second door at around the time she knew I would do. The dog saw me, and behaved in a way as if it hated me. It began to bark snapping its gnashers at me.

H said, "Look what I've got here, and it doesn't like you, the way it's acting."

I said, "You've got another dog. Is it a stray?"

"Doesn't look so to me."

The dog sat, and looking up at H, with its tail wagging along the floor.

"This note was in its collar."

She showed me the note, and I saw what was written there.

I said, "You could be in luck, you just have to wait for its master to come in." I moved closer to H and the dog got angry, got up and started barking.

H said to the dog, "He's a friend, it's ok."

The dog relaxed and went to the side of H.

"It is well trained, I must say," H said, looking repeatedly at the first entrance to see if anyone would enter.

I said, "If no one comes for it, you'll have to take it home."

H said, "I can't do that! It could be somebody else's dog. And this note. It must have an owner. I'll wait and see."

The dog played its part brilliantly. After about twenty minutes the dog left H and went back out through the first entrance. I spent another five minutes with her and then I left through the second door. I walked around and saw my dog sitting there and waiting. I took some food that I had in the bag over my shoulder and gave it to the dog, then I patted it gracefully. The dog had done a great job, very clever indeed. I was surprised that it went off so smoothly.

In the town, I saw a poster. I stopped and had a read. It was about a bible discussion, mainly on the Jews in Egypt. I gave a smile, and noted the time. It starts at 20.00 pm. I'm glad I went to the discussion early because there were many people there. I was seated in one of the chairs close to the stage. The first speaker was an archeologist and what he said went down well. The second speaker was a professor in Old and new Testament studies. I didn't agree with everything he said, but I kept quiet and waited for question time. The last speaker was a writer with a new book out on the "Family of Amenhotep." When the time came for questions, I stood up and asked the professor about Moses. He waffled away a bit then gave me an answer that I was not quite happy with. I didn't ask any more questions, other people did. It was a good meeting altogether but I left still scratching my head. And I'm glad I did not make myself look stupid amongst those experts. There were lots of atheists in the room, and they had asked a number of strange questions.

The following week, I visited H and asked her if the dog had come in again. She said she hadn't seen it. I said to her that she forgot to return a note with the dog. She didn't agree with me. She wasn't going to send a note to some strange person, and especially using a dog. Then I had to tell her that it was me who did all that in order to see how she would take it. She said that she didn't believe it was me, because the dog didn't show any interest in me. I told her that it was well trained. She wouldn't accept that a dog would have been able to keep away from its owner, the way the dog did. I said that it was the truth and that she would see me another time with the dog.

"Any news about your novel," I asked her.

"Not a thing. I'm getting all nervous, waiting to hear news."

"Relax, take it cool."

"I'm trying not to think about it, but it's difficult."

"I'm waiting too, so that I can read it."

"Fingers crossed then, let's hope it's not too long. How about you? Anything new?"

"I went to a discussion about the bible."

"Interesting?"

"In a sort of way. Some things came out which I already knew. Many questions were asked."

"Any dates on the Exodus? Are you still working on them?" H asked.

"To tell you the truth, it is really driving me crazy. It's like walking through a maze and trying to find the way out."

"Is it that bad? I thought you were doing ok!"

"I'm getting on but I have to be careful of where it's leading me to. I have never seen so many dates in all my life."

"What about the Jewish History date?" H wanted to know if I had checked it out.

"I checked that date which is given as 1393 BC for the birth of Moses. If I take away 80 years, I'm left with 1313 BC. This then should be the date of the Exodus. I do not find a New moon here. And it definitely was a new moon when the Israelites left Egypt."

"How did you check it?"

"I drew up a cosmic chart for that year. No new moon."

"Other years?"

"I've got a chart where there's a new moon, but I'm still not sure if it is the right year."

"Keep on trying, don't give in."

"I won't. Something is wrong somewhere. And I'm trying to pick up on what it is."

"From what I have gathered so far, Josephus gives 430 years from the time Abram entered Canaan to the Exodus," H told me. "And he gives 215 years from Jacob entering Egypt to the Exodus."

"You know what I'm trying to do," I said to H. "I'm trying to work with the year that was given for the flood by Josephus. I always have to depend on him because he was given permission to take the scrolls from the temple when it was destroyed in 70 AD."

"And what date is that?" H asked.

"Josephus has given the years from Adam to the flood as 1656 years. He also wrote that from the flood to the birth of Abram was 292 years – Nostradamus gives 295 years."

"But the years Josephus has given are not BC," H reminded me. "How do you transfer 1656 years to BC?"

"There's a converter on the internet. We get a date of 2351 BC for the flood. But as we already know, there are many dates, and we can't be sure which one is correct."

"You've really taken on a hard subject," H warned me. "You could spend your whole life trying to find the right date."

"I believe that I'll get close to it, I just can't give up now. There are many books written on just this one subject."

H said, "So if you add 2351 and 1656 you'll get the date to Adam?"

"Yes," I answered H. "I'll get a date of 4007 BC."

"What about the date of 4004 from the Irish Bishop?"

"Bishop James Ussher, you mean," I asked her. "He started his calculations from Nebuchadnezzar's reign taking genealogies from Adam to Solomon He didn't take the Septuagint bible because it was way out in years compared to the Hebrew bible, at least 1500 years. He had to do careful calculations which were rather complicated. He knew the histories of the other nations. Most of the scholars at the time agreed with his date, 23rd October 4004 BC at Midday."

H said, "I have seen just as you've said that there are many dates recorded."

"I'm glad you've seen what I've got to dig out. Even Freud has given a date for the Exodus."

"And that is?" I said. "He thinks the Exodus took place around 1358 BC-1350 BC."

"So if you draw a chart," H said, "you'd be looking for a new moon? What else do you look for?"

"The chart I draw is called a mundane chart. I can pick out the role of Moses from the 10th house, Israel for the 1st house, the servants of Israel as the 6th house. And because the bible mentioned God, I look to the 9th house."

"That's a lot of work and intuition. Better you than me. I would be totally lost, especially when you talk about charts."

"I know!" I told H, "not everyone is capable of doing that. If I come on to the right one, I'll know immediately. I'll explain it to you another time, H. It is very complex."

"Ok! if you're so sure. But I still don't understand it."

"In time you will, trust me. You're an intelligent person, and you should be able to pick up on it."

"Thanks for the compliment."

"Don't mention it!"

H then asked, "Have you taken Artapanus seriously for mentioning Amenophis; and his story about Moses?"

"I'm still thinking about him," I replied. "I'm not going to push him away just yet" he mentioned Amenophis, but this is Greek, which mean Amenhotep. But which one? There were Amenhotep I, II, III and the IV. The name means 'Amun is satisfied.'"

"I have just picked up a bit on Justin," H told me.

"Justin Martyr," I replied, "was a philosopher, apologist and martyr. He was a Greek and was very important in the early Christian Church. This is what he had to say:"

I will begin then, with our first prophet and lawgiver, Moses; first explaining the times in which he lived, on authorities which among you are worthy of all credit. For I do not propose to prove these things only from our own divine histories, which as yet you are unwilling to credit on account of the inveterate error of your forefathers, but also from your own histories, and such, too, as have no reference to our worship, that you may know that of all your teachers, whether sages, poets, historians, philosophers or lawgivers, by far the oldest, as the Greek historians show us, Moses, who was our first religious teacher.

For in the times of Ogyges and Inachus, whom some of your poets suppose to have been earth-born, Moses is mentioned as the leader and ruler of the Jewish nation. For in this way he is mentioned both by Polemon in the first book of his Hellenics, and by Apion son of Posidonius in his book against the Jews, and in the fourth book of his history, where he says that during the reign of Inachus over Argos the Jews revolted from Amasis King of the Egyptians, and that Moses led them.

And Ptolemaeus the Mendesian, in relating the history of Egypt, concurs in all this. And those who write the Athenian history, Hellanicus and Philochonis (the author of the Attic history), Castor and Thallus and Alexander Polyhistor, and also the very well informed writers on Jewish affairs, Philo and Josephus, have mentioned Moses as a very ancient and time-honored prince of the Jews, Josephus, certainly, desiring to signify even by the title of his work the antiquity and age of the history, wrote thus at the commencement of the history: "The Jewish antiquities of Flavius Josephus," signifying the oldness of the history by the word "antiquities."

And your most renowned historian Diodorus, who employed thirty whole years in epitomizing the libraries, and who, as he himself wrote, travelled over both Asia and Europe for the sake of great accuracy, and thus became an eye-witness of very many things, wrote forty entire books of his own history.

And he in the first book, having said that he learned from the Egyptian priests that Moses was an ancient lawgiver, and even the first, wrote of him in these very words: "For subsequent to the ancient manner of living in Egypt which gods and heroes are fabled to have regulated, they say that Moses first persuaded the people to use written laws, and to live by them; and he is recorded to have been a man both great of soul and of great faculty in social matters." Then having proceeded a little further, and wishing to mention the ancient lawgivers, he mentions Moses first. For he spoke in these words: "Among the Jews they say that Moses ascribed his laws to that God who is called Jehovah

whether because they judged it a marvellous and quite
divine conception which promised to benefit a multitude of
men, or because they were of opinion that the people would
be more obedient when they contemplated the majesty and
power of those who were said to have invented the laws.
And they say that Sasunchis was the second Egyptian
legislator, a man of excellent understanding. And
the third, they say, was Sesonchosis the king, who not
only performed the most brilliant military exploits of
any in Egypt, but also consolidated that warlike race
by legislation. And the fourth lawgiver, they say, was
Bocchoris the king, a wise and surpassingly skilful man.

"So, he's telling us that Moses really existed," H said, "and that he was the leader and lawgiver of the Jews?"

"That's what he actually wrote, just like many other ancient writers."

"You know what?" H frowned, "Some writers, especially some modern ones, just don't believe the story."

"It's always like that, H!" I told her. "Until archaeology proves them wrong."

"What if the whole thing is a facade?" H looked at me more seriously.

"No...I... don't think so." I told her. "The bible is relating what is true. They would not go to all that trouble to make up such lies. The Jews were really in Egypt, and were slaves."

"At least you got me to put questions to you, and to make you think on the subject more deeply, and to come up with some facts."

"That's true," I admitted. "You're really a great help."

"Have you read anything about Nicolas of Damascus?" H asked.

"There you go, coming up with all those ancient writers! Yes, I read a little from him. He was a Greek historian, philosopher, orator and statesman. In his history he wrote that Abram was a foreigner, leading an army from the land of Chaldees to Damascus where he reigned as king and then later went to Canaan with his people. Nicolas wrote that Abram was still honored in the region of Damascus. King David is mentioned, and so is Moses."

"So that settled it then, I mean..."

"I know what you mean! With Moses, we're not in the area of myth any more."

"Then you have solid evidence to go on," H told me. "Moses was the leader of the Jews whether he was Egyptian or Hebrew. And by the way, If he was an Egyptian, he took it upon himself to know all about Abram and the one God."

"Let's stick to what the bible says. Moses was a Levite, a Hebrew."

"There are many modern writers who think otherwise."

"That's good for them," I said, "I've decided that Moses was a Hebrew, adopted by the Pharaoh's daughter, and was in line to take the throne of Egypt."

"Why did he throw it away? Why did he kill the Egyptian? And knowing that the Egyptians hated that kind of behaviour."

H was a bit puzzled.

5

Dates and Chronologies and God

AFTER SOME MORE chat with H, I left. She had lots of boxes to unpack and I guessed they were filled with nothing but books. It was July month and the town were already preparing for the great festival which was held each year in that month. It was the festival of the 'Four Days Marches'. It started way back in 1901. Sometimes when I'm around, I would go to the town and have a look. Other times, I found myself in London.

When I look back at some of the chats H and I had, I found them rather interesting, especially when she would take it on herself and ask me some deep questions. The Exodus is a hard subject. It has baffled many writers researching the subject; and I must say that it's also doing the same to me. But thanks to H, I am able to penetrate deeper, and get to understand what's it all about, and how to finally unravel the mystery of it.

At first, I was upset when I read what Freud wrote, but then, I said, you can't blame him, even if he had it wrong. That is what this task is all about – digging in – and coming out with something that upsets others or with something that pleases them. Some writers think that there are years either misssing or added to the date of the Exodus. I have come to that same conclusion as well. While some are taking 1446 BC as the date for the Exodus, I personally, prefer to stay around the time of Ramesses.

At home, I watched TV, an interesting music show. I forgot about the Exodus for now. I'll come back to it later, I told myself. Now, I'm going to relax, and rest my mind.

The Four Days Marches festival was well on its way. I went to the town every day to have a look seeing that I wasn't going anywhere on holidays. It was that time again when I won't see H for at least four weeks. Sometimes I don't know what I'm thinking about because H is still married. I don't want to get too deep into books and blow my mind at this time. I have to really take it easy, and that is exactly what I did.

The Four Days Marches came to an end and it wasn't long before H was back at work.

We greeted each other and asked how the holidays went down. H said that she didn't go anywhere special. She had stayed at home doing things around the home. meeting friends, taking the dogs out for long walks. As for myself, I told her I too took things easy. Now I feel that I could take on the world. The energy in me was brewing up, and ideas, new ones kept on creeping in my mind. H was pleased to hear that everything was ok with me.

I said to her, "I'm ready to tackle the Exodus now that I'm full of energy. I will pick a date and keep to it no matter what."

"That's good to hear," H said. "Soon you'll be coming to the end. Is that right?"

"You're not far wrong. I'll finish the Exodus and get on to something new."

"Like what?"

"Oh! I have so many plots in my head. I'll see what I come up with."

"When you finish the book, I'll have to read it slowly." H told me. "Its not like a romance novel where you can read through it and understanding what's it all about. The Exodus is a deep subject. Very complex and sometimes confusing."

"That I already know, H," I said. "But seeing that I took it on myself to research it, I shall have to go through all the deep waters, and come out without being bitten by some dangerous fish."

H said, "All those chronologists, they all work with different dates."

"There are quite a lot of them. I'll just mention a few. Sextus Jullius Africanus was a Christian historian around 2nd and 3rd centuries. He gives us some years, like from Moses to the first Olympiad, there were 1020 years. The first Olympiad began in 776 BC, so if we add 1020 years, we get 1796 BC, the time of Moses. Some of the chronologies are way out, and we cannot take them seriously. All I can do is check and see what I come up with."

"Have you check this one yet?" H asked.

"I've got it written down along with the others to check them later."

"You'll let me know what you find, won't you?"

"Of course! H, I won't keep you in the dark, seeing that you have become really serious about my work, and encouraging me along."

"You really know how to rub it in, dont you?"

"Just complimenting you for backing me up."

"Carry on with your chronologists."

"There was also George Syncellus. "Syncellus" was not his real name, but given by the early Church to monks and clerks who were close with their bishops, and served as deacons in offices of the mass, and would take over from the bishop at his death. George the Syncellus retired to a monastery and wrote the "Selection of Chronology. His work starts from the creation of the world according to biblical account, and down to the Roman emperor Diocletian."

"You're going to find dates that don't match up to the actual date of the flood," H explained. "Some of them are going to be out by at least hundreds of years."

"I've already met with a few. But as I've already said, I'm looking for the date of the Exodus with a new moon. I'm going to come against quite a lot. I need deep inspiration. I've got to be in a place that's harmonic and peaceful."

"That's interesting," H said, "working in a place that's unharmonic is not good. You have to find a spot where the vibrations are good."

"That I know for sure. You're absolutely right."

"I read a bit about Jerome," H said. "What's his chronology saying?"

"St. Jerome Hyronymus used the chronology of Eusebius. He wrote about the Roman writers. He has given data from Abraham to events that took place; and mentioning the years of the Olympiads. Both his works and that of Eusebius was lost, luckily, they found the Armenian translation."

"If we had the originals from all those ancient writers, what a treasure that would have been!" H said enthusiastically.

"I know! but that's the way life is – losing and discovering. Let's be glad that we got a few words from what they wrote."

"Now that chronologist M Scotus," H said, "he set the creation date to 1st October 4004 BC."

"Of course," I said, "he tried to correct the dates that Ussher set down, but he kept the same year. The date of 23rd October was a Julian working; he said that it came out as 21st September on the Gregorian Calendar. This Gregorian Calendar came about through pope Gregory 13th. The Julian Calendar makes a year as 365.25 days, and is eleven minutes less than the Gregorian."

"This Julian Calendar is from Julius Caesar, then?" H asked.

"It was devised when he came into power."

"What about the Hebrew Calendar?"

"They used to have September/October as their first month, but changed it to March/April when they departed from Egypt."

"So they had a lunar Calendar?" H was digging in deeper, wanting to know all the facts."

"A correction had to be made when we came to the Solar Calendar. They changed their Calendar because God had told them to do so."

"So how do you stand now knowing all these things? Are you any closer to the Exodus date?" H inquired.

"I'm getting there slowly, I have to carefully sift through all the information I have noted down, and to backtrack a few times, but it's all coming out ok."

"I'm glad it's working out for you," she said as she turned to serve a customer. "Just one moment!"

After the customer left, she came back to me, and said "You already know that I'm not such a deep believer as yourself, but I'm always here and willing to help."

"That I already know. You've helped a great deal, believer or not. And you came out with some good questions that would have stumped any expert. keep up the good work."

"There's a spark of something deep down inside of me, but when it comes to all this talk about God, I'm really baffled. Who is this God?" H was serious now. She wanted answers.

I said, "Through my research with the Exodus, I found that the God of the Israelites came down on the mountain of Sinai. The mountain was covered in smoke for six days, and on the 7th day, God called Moses to come to him."

"How do we know that that is true. Because it is written doesn't mean that it is true!"

"Moses recorded in his writings what happened. He wasn't telling any lies. The people were a part of what happened. Moses got commands from God, and he passed them on to the Israelites."

"Some writers believe it was a volcano."

"Oh! No! H, It couldn't be a volcano. Who would take people up a mountain where a volcano is active? And anyway, there was no volcano recorded in that area. There was that volcano 'Thera', and some people are trying to say, or have said, that it had to do with the Exodus."

"So you think that God came from another solar system?"

"Wherever he came from, he actually landed on Mount Sinai and spoke with Moses and the Israelites out of a cloud and fire. The 70 elders, Moses, Aaron and his twos sons went up the mountain. Moses alone was allowed to enter to God, the rest had to stay back at a distance. The people weren't allowed to come near, even the priests had to stay back or God would break out upon them."

"Break out upon them?" H asked. "How was he going to do that?"

"Moses said that God was a devouring fire. He landed on the mountain in fire. I think that there's something really mysterious that we as normal people would not be able to understand."

"Can we then take that as solid proof for the existence of God?" H asked.

"It sounds solid enough for me."

"What did he tell the Israelites?"

"He told them that he was their God; that he was the one who brought them out of Egypt, out of the land of slavery. He told them that he was the God of Abraham, Isaac and Jacob; and that he had made a promise on oath to give them the land of Canaan."

"That sounds ok to me," H said. "God proved to them that he was God."

"Well you see," I started to tell H, "He not only proved to them that he was God, he fought their battles for them as well But the Israelites were stubborn, they abandoned God many times, and went and followed other nations, worshipping idols of stone, wood, iron, silver, brass, clay and gold."

"The bible says that Moses talked with God face to face. How is that posiible when no one can see God and live?"

"H," I said, "you have many good questions, and I'll try to answer them according to what is written in the Old Testament including the New Testament. Moses did not see God face to face, as I'm seeing you now. The bible said that God came down in a cloud and this happened at the entrance to the Tent of Meeting. God of course, speaking to Moses from within the cloud."

"That sounds like a very interesting passage. I'll come back to you on that later. I have to unpack all these boxes and label the books. We shall talk some more later on."

I left the bookshop, giving H time to digest what I had said. There were quite a number of boxes there unopened, and I knew she would be very busy for some time. One thing I must say though, H took it upon herself to encourage me, and then to listen to what I had to say about the book I was writing. She really is a one. I could babble along about things she doesn't know anything of; and calmly and patiently, she would roll her eyes over and give me that look, telling me that that was enough. It was a good sign, and I would immediately change the subject, and then she's relieved. She wasn't going to come right out and say "Stop! my head is expanding, it's going to blow." She had that way with her blue deep lovely eyes, of giving the signal to ease off when it got too deep. I took the signal seriously and next time I saw her we spoke of simple matters, every day business, what's taking place in the town, and of course, new adventures. H, I saw would make a good teacher. When I was back in my school in the early years, I used to pick out the teachers who were really first class, and I got it right every time. She had told me she was only doing the teaching job as part-time. I tried to make her see if she could get to teach for longer periods – that would be great – and more enjoyable.

When I saw H again, she told me things weren't going as she had hoped them to. The publishers weren't making up their minds if they want to publish her material or not. She had gotten a few poems published in a group magazine. Again, I told her, do not worry too much, things would work themselves out in the end.

"What about your book? How is it coming on?" she asked me.

"It is pushing on fine. Just have to look up a few more chronologies, and take some more notes."

"So you have your own chronology ready?"

I answered: "Yes, I'm working on one. There are a few things I have to sort out. By the way, I have drawn the chart of yourself and children."

"What have they to say?"

"Quite a lot! very interesting details."

H asked: "How can a chart tell a human being what's going to happen? Is it all planned already?"

I said, "The human being has free will. He can make choices. He can be free to do whatever he wants to do, but there are some natural laws, that cannot be avoided. The individual has to bear the consequencies."

"Tell me what you see!"

"I'll start for you from the beginning. I'll keep it short!"

"Ok!"

I said to H, explaing quite clearly, "You're a Leo from the sun. At the time you were born, the sun was passing through the zodiac sign of Leo. And at the rising point which is your ascendant, the sign of Scorpio is there. Your moon is in the sign of Cancer. From these three things a lot can be known about your personality. A Leo loves children, entertainment and sports, and is just like a lion in the community. A scorpio is a lover of things that are deep, such things to do with the other world. Scorpios are sexy. Cancers are home loving, sensitive and protective."

"I must say," H began, "you've hit on some points that are true. But tell me what you see for three years from now."

"I see the planet of love, Venus, moving from retrograde movement to direct. The planet is making a trine aspect to your ascendant. This trine aspect is positive. It is a time when love and beauty will function, and the love feelings would flow freely."

"And if it doesn't happen?" H inquired. "What then?"

"Oh!" I said, "you can bet your life that it will come about just as I have explained it to you."

"Then it means that I cannot avoid it."

"H," I said, "we're only human beings and there are lots of unexplianed things that has us baffled. I'm afraid that astrology is one of them. You mention earlier that the birth time has to do with telling what is to come."

"Yes, that's true. The birth time is very important, especially if it's accurate. From it we can go back to the past, and also forward to the future. If you have accurate information about your grandparents, I could check and tell you quite a number of things."

"Ok!" H said, "you've convinced me a bit, but I am still sceptical. I fail to see how those planets up there could tell us what to do."

"They're not telling what you have to do, they're just timing events that are to take place."

"Events?"

"That's right! Like when you meet someone and fall in love."

"Come on! How could that be? I do not have to wait for the planets to tell me when to fall in love? I can fall in love any time I want to."

"No you can't! If that was so, it would make no sense telling you about astrology. The fact is: when the right time comes around, you fall in love."

"I still get the idea that every thing is already planned in advanced."

"I appears so, but we still have the last say."

H asked: "How do you work that one out? You just stated that at a certain time we have to go through certain events!"

"What ever happens, human beings has free will."

H wasn't satisfied. "It is a very complicated system, then? You cannot say for sure if a certain event will take place."

"I've never yet heard of anyone who avoided having a child, if their chart says that they'll have one. Some things can be avoided, and others not."

"I still can't get over it that the planets has such power," H said. "It is really a baffling thing, and many people have already abandoned the idea that the planets are in control."

"I don't know about in control, but there's surely some connection between them and us."

"Take a star that is 864 light years away! How in God's name can that star affect someone on earth?"

"H," I said to her, "I tell you it does. There are many things that we cannot comprehend, and yet they're there and working."

She said, "I must admit that that is true."

I said to her, "I've decided now to take a year and stick with it. I mean a year of the Exodus."

"So you're almost at the end now," she said. "You've done quite a lot of research!"

"And where has it got me? Hanging round the 19th dynasty of the Egyptian kings. And every day I keep repeating that one passage. It says, *After a long time the king of Egypt died.*"

"So you're hoping it's Ramesses II?"

"Who else can it be?" I replied. "We know that Pepi II ruled about 90 years making him the longest ruling king in ancient Egypt. But that is way out."

"Could it be then the son of Ramesses II, Merneptah?" H asked.

"I've a strong feeling that it was him. Anyway, I'll set down my chronological dates." I told her.

6

My own Exodus dates

"START JOTTING DOWN those dates, then. If they're wrong, they're wrong. At least you've tried, that can't be bad." H told me. "Stick to Merneptah."

"Ok! I set Moses as being born 1316 BC. And you know what? There's only three years different between what is recorded in the Jewish history and my date.. I have also another date which I got by adding 200 years."

"Wow! Why 200?" H wanted to know. She couldn't follow me now. She looked lost.

"This is because of the feeling that some years are missing."

"Oh! I see! Why couldn't it be 300 or more?" she asked.

"Let's not go haywire, eh! 200 years is about right."

"That would bring the other date to around 1598 BC or thereabout."

I said, "I'll draw a chart and see what I could find. That would be really interesting."

"You have to have a new moon, is that right?" H asked.

"Absolutely! That's what I need to have in the chart. I will start at the year 1236 BC for the Exodus."

"Around the time of Merneptah?"

"Yes," I said. "The bible said: *'after many days the king of Egypt died.'* I take this to be Seti I. And again, the bible said, *'after a long time the king of Egypt died.'* I take this to be Ramesses II. So the Exodus must have been in the reign of Merneptah."

"Only one thing still bothers me," H explained. "Neither

Seti I or Ramesses II could be the King of Egypt who ordered the Hebrew children to be killed. They both had sons. We need to find a king who hadn't had a son."

"We've been all through that. And if I think about it too much, my head will blow." I told her. "So let me carry on. Moses would then be born in 1316 BC."

"From your dates, the Israelites crossed the Jordan 1196 BC," H told me.

"I feel they had to enter the land when no Egyptian forces were in control there."

"These are your first dates, I suppose."

"I have another set of dates, and I'll let you see them later."

"It would mean that Joseph died in 1486 BC, and born in 1596 BC. He went down to Egypt or I must say, was sold to the Egyptians around 1579 BC," H reminded me. "He was 30 when he stood before the Pharaoh. That would be in 1566 BC."

"Thank you very much, H. The dates are correct. Jacob came down with his family in 1557 BC. He was 130 years old so he was born in 1687 BC. Isaac would be born around 1747 BC just after the destruction of Sodom and Gomorrah. Abraham then, would be born in 1847 BC."

H said, "If I do some adding, I get the year 1922 BC when Abraham entered Canaan."

"Correct. And if we add 292 years to the birth of Abraham we get 2139 BC for the flood. We need to add 600 years to the flood and we get the birth of Noah. If we add 1656 years to the flood we get the creation of Adam, which would be 3795 BC. This gives 34 years more than the Jewish year of 3761 BC."

I said, "If we add 2139 BC to 600, we get 2739 BC, the year of the birth of Noah."

"So we can plot all the dates if we wanted to?"

"I'm only taking the main ones. The next dates I'm going

to show you, bring us right into the 15th dynasty of 1650 BC-1550 BC."

"Are you satisfied with the chart you've drawn?" H asked.

"I am. It has a few interesting points. One of the main one is the New Moon."

"Anything else?"

"Yes. I'm looking at the house of enemies, and to see what the ruler of that house is doing."

"Trust me to be asking you questions about that science where I know nothing of it!" H said.

"That's true," I told her. "It is good of you to be asking questions."

"So you've also made a list of the Jewish dates?"

"Here they are." I showed her a list that I had on me.

According to the Old Testament, the Jewish Calendar, these are the dates:

Adam and Eve	3760 BC
Seth born	3630
Enosh born	3525
Kenan born	3435
Mahalelel	3365
Jered	3300
Enoch	3138
Methusaleh	3074
Lamech	2886
Adam dies	2831
Noah born	2704
Shem born	2203
Flood	2150
Terah born	1882

H said, "It is very interesting but it is not at all accurate."

I told her, "Everyone has their own dates. Now my dates for 1598 BC are also not accurate, but are the dates I came up with."

"It is better to have dates that makes some sense, and that are close and not way out by hundreds of years." H told me.

The time for holidays was coming around again and I know that soon H would be off for four weeks. There's nothing I can do about it but just wait until she comes back. In the meantime I just had to try and check that the information I had is ok. I looked again at the chart for 1236 BC. It has Capricorn rising with the ruler Saturn in the 6th house conjuncting the 6th house. The chart is an event chart and so the ascendant is Israel. The 6th house is the servants and workers. I have quite a lot to tell H when I see her again.

After the holidays were over, I met up with H again and began to talk about things that had happened. H told me that she went touring with a group of poets through the land for ten days. She showed me some pictures.

"Did you enjoy the experience?" I asked her.

"Oh!" She answered. "I felt as though I was there before. Strange, isn't it?"

"At least you're back safely. That's what happens when we go on holidays. We have to come back and face the old routine."

"What about you? How's your research going? Found anything new?"

"I could raise my head and cry out. All those dates keep rushing at me. Remember I told you I'm going to keep to my own dates, I could be wrong."

"Oh, no. All the work you have done. What's the problem there?" H asked.

I said to her, "I told you I need to add about 200 years to the dates that I found. Well, I'm scratching my head. Reading some more, I have come up with Ahmose I. I know what you're going to say: 'I'm going all over the place.' I've got to hold the horses, and don't let them run loose."

"Wasn't Ahmose's wife Nefertari?" H asked.

"Yes, She was Queen Nefertari."

"Then Moses could have been around that time?"

"Good try, H, but I think somewhere around where they had sixty kings serving," I explained to her.

"Ahmose had a son," H told me. "And he had a brother too, Kamose was the name. They both fought against the Hyksos."

"That's true. The son of Ahmose was Amenhotep I, his sister was Sitamun. I don't think that Moses fit in here. The one thing we're are looking for is a king without a son."

H said, "So you still feel that the Artapanus story is true. Are you going to look through those kings?"

"You know what? I've been thinking very deeply about Joseph. If I could only get the date that he went down to Egypt, everything else would just fall into place. What about Pepi who took the throne over when he was still young; and remember, Joseph told his brothers that God made him a father to the king. There are two things that I'm trying to unravel here," I told H.

"What are they?" she asked.

I said to her, "The king who took Joseph on, had a son. Later that king died, and his son took over. I want to know who they were. It seems to me that this all happened within the new kingdom."

"What dates have you got for that?" H asked.

"As we already know," I told her, "there are many dates. If I start from about 1570 BC to 1090 for the New kingdom, I think that would be okay."

"I read somewhere," H said, "that Moses grew up with the king's sons in the royal house."

"Yes, I read about that too. So we have to look as well for a king with sons."

"Could you not get a line on what Josephus wrote?" H asked. "It would be nice to experiment with those dates that he has given."

"I got them written down. He said that the temple was built 147 years before Carthage was founded. Well we know, according to legend that Carthage was founded by the Phoenician Queen Elissa in about 813 BC."

"So that would give us a date of 960 BC thereabouts," H said. "If we add 480 years to that we get 1440 BC for the Exodus."

I said to H, "I'm not satisfied with that date. I don't think that they stayed that long in Egypt."

"No harm checking it though. You said it has to be a New Moon, but what if they came out when there was no New Moon?" H asked.

"I doubt that," I told her. "One thing that I have found out, the Israelites were always busy with the New Moon. It has to be a New Moon when they came out."

"Have you done any check with this Inachus?" she asked.

"I did poke my nose in that area, most of it could be myth, but I'm still trying to dig something out."

H said, "This Inachus was supposed to be a king, and there's a river named after him."

I said, "You are right there. Moses was supposed to be living around the same time as him." I told her, "I came up with a date of 1860 BC."

"Are you going to see what you can get from that date? H asked.

"I think I shall put it aside for now," I said. "Something has just come into my mind."

"What is that?"

"You know, the Egyptians kings weren't called 'Pharaoh' until around 1500 BC."

"So?"

"Well," I said, "we are dealing with kamose and Ahmose, the two brothers who defeated the Hyksos."

"I'm not following you here," H said. "Explain some more to me."

"Can't you see? They drove out the Hyksos who were known as Shepherds. They weren't going to let any Shepherds back in."

"Now you've got me completely lost."

"Ahmose re-united Egypt, and that means there were no enemies left in Egypt to cause trouble," I told her.

"Okay! Now I've got you!" she said.

"I'm now coming to my senses and sticking with the New Kingdom," I told her.

"What dates have you got for that?"

"My dates range between 1530 and 1050. Somewhere between these dates was the Exodus."

"I read that Joseph told his brothers to tell the Pharaoh that they were shepherds," H said to me. "It seems that the Pharaoh was interested in shepherds. He even gave them a piece of land, Goshen."

"I don't think Ahmose would have done that after kicking the Hyksos out. Some think it refers to a group of Asiatic people who came and took over half of Egypt," I said. "One of the things I'm thinking about is the fact that the Egyptians didn't allow any foreigner to take the crown."

"What about the Amenhotep family?" H said.

"What about them?" I asked. "Amenhotep III was known for making alliances with foreign women. I got the feeling that Akhenaten could have been the son of a Hittite woman."

"There are some who think he was an Israelite," H told me.

"You're joking! That would mean that the Israelites had control of the Egyptian throne. If that was so, it would have been written in the bible."

H said, "We already know that Joseph was Governor over all Egypt, the Hyksos did not have control over all of Egypt."

"You're becoming very clever, H, I have to watch myself here. But I like it if you are that clever, it urges me on."

"Well is it true or not?"

H was waiting for an answer.

7

Amenhotep III and His Family

"IT IS WELL known," I said to H, "that Amenhotep III was very friendly with some of the nations around him, and took one or two foreign princesses in his household."

"That is true," H said. "His wife Tiye has the features of a Nubian or African, and she could have been a princess from one of those places."

"One thing I know is that she turned out to be the most powerful Queen in Egypt."

H said, "I thought Hatshepsut had that title!"

"Ah! that's where many people are wrong. Hatshepsut was a Pharaoh, not a Queen," I told H.

"I know a little bit of history, "H said, "but not like you. You know quite a lot."

"But still don't know enough," I told her.

"Right! So Thuthmose IV was Amenhotep's father?"

"Yes."

"Amenhotep was not really a bad Pharaoh, he did Egypt well. He held on to the ancient religion for a long time. And as you must have heard, the ancient Egyptians worshipped many gods. It was the sun god Aten that Amenhotep turned to in his later years."

"The influence was passed over to his son, who really became a fanatic," I told her.

H said, "Okay, so why do some people think that Tiye was an Israelite?"

"I pass quickly over those stories because if they were true we would have read them in the bible," I said.

"But what if—?"

I broke in quickly.

"The Israelites didn't want to have anything to do with the Egyptians? I'm sure they would have been proud of the fact that they had the Egyptian crown for themselves, which was called 'The Amarna Period.'"

"So Akhenaten didn't have an Israrelite upbringing?" H asked. "Are you saying he got his monotheism from his father?"

"Yes, he inherited it. But let's not forget his mother. She wasn't Egyptian, and he would also inherit something from her."

"I think he went a bit too far breaking away from the ancient way of life," H said. "He had much problems with the Amun priests of Egypt. He finally moved away, and went up to the desert to build his own complex."

"He went completely mad on this 'Aten', nothing was greater than it. He wrote hymns to it."

"I read somewhere," H told me, "that Psalm 104 is like one of his hymns."

"I personally do not think that all of Psalm 104 comes from a hymn of Akhenaten. I agree, there are bits and pieces that sound like one of his hymns, but not the total Psalm," I told her.

"What about his daughters, he had six of them. Do you know anything about them?" H asked.

"It is recorded that he had six daughters. Meritaten was the first born, and her mother was the Great Royal wife Nefertiti. Then there was Anchesena, Neferneferu, Maketaten, Ankhesenpaaten Tasherit, and Setepenre. Akhenaten's sons were Tutankhamun and Smenhkare. There's some sort of mystery about Smenhkare. Some think that he was not of royal blood."

"That's rather strange," H told me. "For Nefertiti had disappeared suddenly, and some think that she came back as Smenhkare. But it is very hard to get into this ancient Egyptian history."

"What ever happened, Smenhkare took the throne after he married Meritaten. First Akhenaten had to finish his time, then Tutankhamun took over, then Smenhkare, and then Aye. I think that both Aye and Horemheb were looking after Tutankhamun."

H said, "Tutankhamun when he took over the throne went by the name Tutankhaten, and then later changed over to Tutankhamun."

"You're right, he was then influenced by the ancient priests who resided at Thebes."

"I think that if Nefertiti was the mother of Tutankhamun, he would not have changed his name, and he would have followed in his father's footsteps worshipping the Aten fully." H told me.

Soon H will be off again on her holidays, and I won't be seeing her again for six weeks when we could discuss some more about some ancient history, mainly, Egypt and the Exodus. H has done me pretty well seeing that she is not really into history as deep as myself. She is busy with her book, and soon it will get published and I could sit back and read it.

We had a last talk about Ankhesenpaaten, the third daughter of Akhenaten and Nefertiti.

"Ankhesenpaaten was the wife of Tutankhamun," H said to me.

"Where did you pick that one up," I said. "You're absolutely right. Her name means, 'she lives with the Aten,' or 'she lives through the Aten.' She changed her name to Ankhesenamun."

"Both she and Tutankhamun were forced to change back to

the old way of worship in Egypt." H told me.

"You know why that was," I said to her. "It was that Aye who was in control. He was persecuting the followers of the Aten. He and Horemheb had their eyes on being Pharaoh."

"I thought the throne was only among the royal family, and no commoner to get hold of it," H said.

"That's true. It is said that Aye was a commoner, the son of an Egyptian priest. For him to become Pharaoh, he had to marry someone of royal status," I told her.

"You know something," H said to me, "Aye was the grandfather of Ankhesenpaaten. She was told she had to marry him when her husband Tutankhamun died. In trying to prevent such a thing happening, she wrote a letter to the Hittites, asking them to send one of their sons to Egypt. The ancient Egyptians were very tight with their royalty, so that didn't happen. In the end she had to marry Aye."

"What happened to her in the end?" I wanted to see if H was up to date.

"She just disappeared. Her body was not found. It still is a mystery.

"Do you think Aye or Horemheb had something to do with it?" I asked.

"It is possible! Either Aye or Horemheb could have done something to her, who knows?" H told me.

"At one time I was thinking of putting the Exodus in the time of Aye. I change my mind. I will stick to the year 1236," I told her.

"Well, you've been plotting years, and you have finally decided to stick with 1236 BC. Now suppose I tell you that I have a year as well," H said.

"What's that? What year have you got? You really surprise me here," I told her.

"It is 1339 BC, and don't ask me too many questions why this is the year."

"H, I have to ask questions, I'm a researcher, and they do ask lots of questions. You've come up with a year when Amenhotep IV was in power. That's amazing, that's *interesting*."

We left off talking about the Amenhotep III family. H was off from work for six long weeks, when she comes back we could dig in some more to see what we can find.

H is back from her holidays; she had a great time, and is still looking her best. I missed her, and is glad that she's back safely. I'll let her have a little rest then we can start thrashing out this Exodus thing.

H asked me what I had been doing while she was away. I told her I was just taking it easy. I learned from her that she had some work accepted among other writers. That was great news. H was very good with the language, and I have tried my best many times, to make her bring out the best that's inside of her. I like her style of writing.

8

Final Dates and Conclusion

"THAT DATE YOU have given to me, I find it very interesting," I said to H. "The date of 1339 BC. I had a look through the astronomical workings, and sure enough, there are six planets in the sign of Aries. Using the date of 14th of April, I'm looking for a New Moon because the Israelites came out of Egypt when it was dark."

H said, "I thought they were kicked out the land?"

"Of course, that's what took place. They didn't even have time to prepare food properly."

"Coming back to Akhenaten," H told me, "I read somewhere that he went to the Sinai with some of his followers – about 600."

"H," I said, "you have to be careful with what you read. He had to abdicate from the pressure the Amun priests put on him. Probably that's why he left Thebes and went to Amarna. But those who want to make Akhenaten into Moses, have to think again. Akhenaten died in Egypt, Moses died in Sinai."

"That Amenhotep III's family is rather interesting," H said. "A lot of strange things have happened in it. But I must say though, Amenhotep and his wife Tiye worked together and kept Egypt strong."

"Yes, I too find it rather interesting. But we are here dealing with ancient Egypt. The Royal family was tight, it was not easy for a commoner to get the crown."

"This Sitamun, daughter of Amenhotep married her own

father, and she was Princess and Queen, and had quite a few titles. One of them was 'King's Great Wife,'" H told me.

"You know what I still have in my head?" I ask H.

"Something you're working on?"

"It's that Artapanus with his writings about Moses," I said to her. "Artapanus is driving me bonkers He reckons that it was the wife of Akhenaten who rescued Moses and brought him to her father Amenhotep. I know that Nefertiti was the wife of Akhenaten, along with some others, one being Kiya."

"But suppose Artapanus is right about Moses living in the household of Amenhotep III."

"That's possible," I said. "But we are looking for a princess who is also a queen. We're looking for a king who has no son. Moses is the one who will take over. Someone thinks that Amenemhat III is the king, and his daughter Sobekneferu is the princess who saved Moses. She was also a queen. Amenemhat had no son."

"She doesn't carry the name of 'Merris' or 'Thurmuthis' or 'Bathia,'" H said.

"I know," I told her. "But I had to sift through everything, then make up my mind. Talking about dates, that bring us back to the reign of Seti I."

"Oh, yeah! Let's hear what you have to say," H said.

"I have to stick with Seti I and Ramesses II, all because of what the bible said. The Israelites built store cities, Pithom, which means 'Per-Atum, the sun god of Heliopolis.' Also Ramesses. Don't forget that the ancient Egyptians worshipped many gods."

"Let's see these dates," H said.

"The Egyptian dates I came across are these:"

```
Ahmose ........................................................ 1550-1525
Amenhotep 1 ................................................ 1525-1504
Thutmose 1 .................................................. 1504-1492
Thutmose 2 .................................................. 1492-1479
Queen Hatshepsut with Thutmose 1472-1457; 1479-1425
Amenhotep 2 ................................................ 1425-1399
Thutmose 4 .................................................. 1399-1389
Amenhotep 3 ................................................ 1389-1351
Akhenaten(Amenhotep 4) .......................... 1351-1337
Smenkhkare ................................................ 1336-1334
Tutankhamun .............................................. 1334-1325
Aye .............................................................. 1325-1321
Horemheb ................................................... 1321-1292
Ramses 1 ..................................................... 1292-1290
Seti 1 .......................................................... 1290-1279
Ramesses 2 .................................................. 1279-1213
Merenptah .................................................. 1213-1203
```

"We already know that there are many dates. So what now?" H asked.

"I have taken 1236 BC because it has a New Moon, and because I saw certain things inside the chart that could account for what the bible said. I found that:"

```
Horemheb reigned from ........................... 1361-1333
Ramese 1 ..................................................... 1333-1332
Seti 1 .......................................................... 1332-1317
Moses was born in the reign of Seti 1 ..................... 1316
Ramesses .................................................... 1317-1250
Merneptah .................................................. 1250-1240
```

"I do hope that it is the right one," H said. "You have done a lot of research. Do you feel very confident about it?"

"Well, yes! I picked this one because it is for midnight on the 14th April. Moses wrote in his notes that they left Ramesses on the 15th of the first month. In the cosmic map, God is represented by the 9th house, the planet Pluto is there in the 8th house, its own house. Pluto is also ruler of the 11th house which gives a connection of 11th and 9th houses. This has to do with long distance travel, space, foreign countries. But I shall not tell you too much about this because I know you know nothing about it."

"You're right there," H said. "It would be like talking another language to me."

"That is right what you said because if someone was talking about physics to me, of which I know nothing, I too, would not understand."

"But that's okay," H said. "What conclusion have you come to now?"

"Well it's been great fun and excitement researching the Exodus. There's still something very mysterious. Although I've come up with this date, it could be out by so many years, but I'm glad I had the guts to get in there and do it. I'm always getting the feeling that Amenhotep III could have been the Pharaoh, and if not we find ourselves going into the 1700's according to Artapanus. The Israelites were definitely in Egypt. Joseph had power as governor, and Moses was a prince with the chance of being Pharaoh."

"I think you have done a good job, and you didn't give up," H said.

"I have to congratulate you, and give you all the thanks in the world for standing your ground, and putting all those questions to me. You're a fine woman."

Other books by John Gumbs:

Jehanne
The Burning of Jehanne